Herbert S. Zim
DIAMONDS

Illustrated by Gustav Schrotter

WILLIAM MORROW & COMPANY INC.

New York   1959

The author wishes to thank Henry P. Chandler,
analyst, U.S. Bureau of Mines, for checking the
manuscript and art work of this book.

8   9   10   75

There are gems more valuable than diamonds. There are gems more brilliant and more beautiful. But the diamond is still the most popular, most unusual, and most interesting gem of all. And this is true in spite of the fact that diamonds are nothing but carbon.

Of the hundred or more chemical elements, a few are common throughout the entire universe. Hydrogen and helium are in our sun and in billions upon billions of stars. Carbon, however, is much less common. Even here on earth there is not much of it. The total quantity forms less than one per cent of the rocks we know. Still, this amounts to billions of tons.

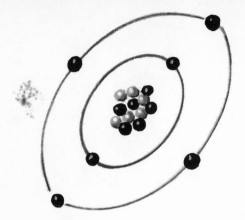

A carbon atom has
6 protons, 6 neutrons,
and 6 electrons.

oxygen	46.5%
silicon	27.6
aluminum	8.1
iron	5.1
magnesium	2.1
calcium	3.6
sodium	2.8
potassium	2.6
titanium	0.6
CARBON	0.1
other elements	0.9
	Total 100.0%

Carbon is a unique element. It is found in all living things and, as far as we know, life without carbon is impossible. Every plant and animal, from the smallest moss to the great sequoia trees and from the tiny shrew, which weighs less than a dime, to the mammoth whale, has carbon in its body.

least shrew

haircap moss

Much of the carbon found in the rocks of the earth has come from living things. Such carbon is found in coal, oil, and limestone. Deposits of carbon form very slowly and are not very common.

blue whale, world's largest animal

sequoia, world's largest tree

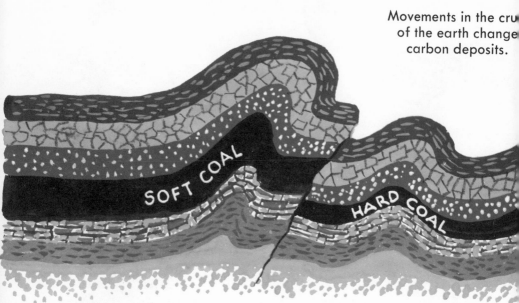

Movements in the cru
of the earth change
carbon deposits.

SOFT COAL

HARD COAL

Sometimes heat and pressure in the crust of the earth change carbon deposits until the carbon begins to form crystals. The name of this soft, dark, greasy, crystallized carbon is graphite. When we use it in pencils we call it lead. Under even more heat and pressure carbon is crystallized still further. Then it may become an unusual bluish-white sparkling stone—the best of all gems and the most prized: the diamond.

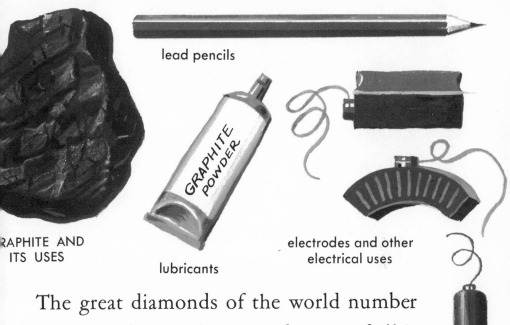

lead pencils

GRAPHITE POWDER

RAPHITE AND
ITS USES

lubricants

electrodes and other
electrical uses

The great diamonds of the world number
about three dozen. The most famous of all is
the Cullinan, discovered in 1905 in a South
African mine owned by Sir Thomas Cullinan,
for whom the stone was named. The Cullinan
diamond weighed 3106 carats—over a pound

linan diamond,
jest ever found

natural size

and a quarter. The mining company sold the rough stone to the Transvaal government, and the government presented it to King Edward VII on his 66th birthday. From London the gem was sent to Amsterdam, where the best diamond cutters spent months studying how to split, cut, and polish this magnificent stone.

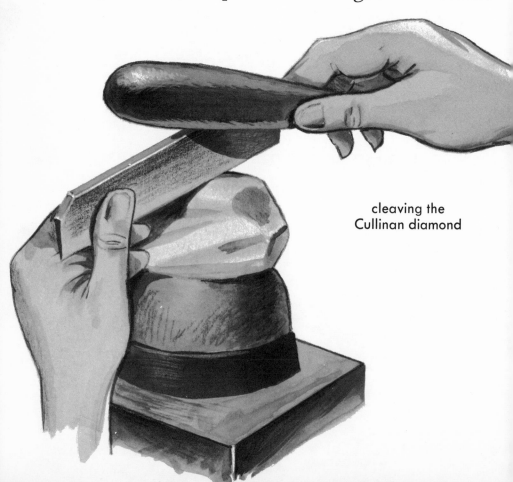

cleaving the
Cullinan diamond

The responsibility for the cutting rested on a single man. On February 10, 1908, he placed his steel blade at the exact spot for dividing the diamond and gave it a sharp blow. The cleaving blade broke, but the stone was un-touched. At the second tap, the diamond split exactly right. Later the Cullinan diamond was split again and again, to produce 9 large gems and 96 smaller ones weighing 1063 carats.

the royal
scepter of
Great Britain

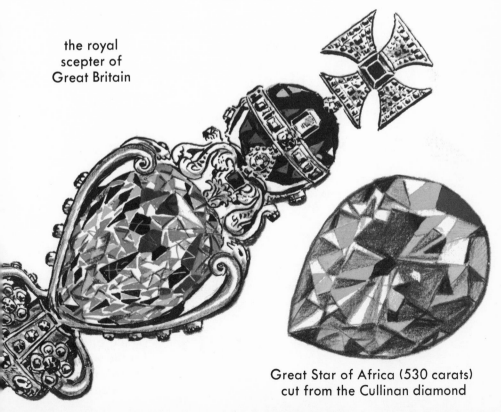

Great Star of Africa (530 carats)
cut from the Cullinan diamond

The largest of these Cullinan gems is the Great Star of Africa. Weighing 530 carats, this largest cut diamond in the world rests in the royal scepter. It may be viewed in the Tower of London. The other Cullinan stones are also part of the British crown gems. During World War II, so the story goes, the gems were taken from their settings, sealed in jars, and safely buried in a potato field.

Another great African diamond is the Excelsior, weighing 995 carats. Before the Cullinan was found, this was the world's largest. Later it was cut into 21 gems, the largest weighing 70 carats. In 1934 the Jonker diamond (726

WEIGHT OF DIAMONDS

100 points = 1 carat

1 carat = .2 gram or 200 milligrams

142 carats = 1 ounce

The carat once stood for the weight of the seed of a tropical locust tree.

carats) was found only a few miles from where the Cullinan was discovered, in a mudbank after a rainstorm. The Jonker yielded several gems; the largest, weighing 125 carats, belonged to the king of Egypt. Also from Africa came the great Jubilee diamond, 650 carats in the rough.

AFRICAN DIAMONDS

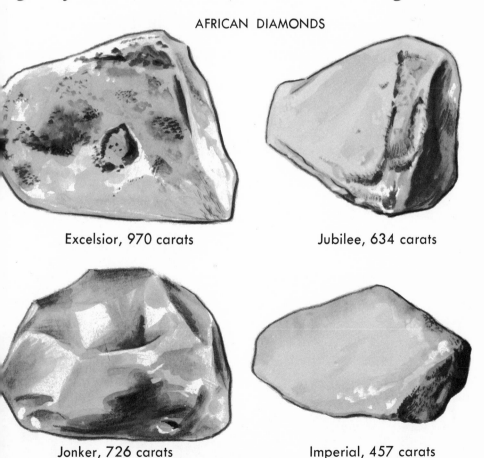

Excelsior, 970 carats

Jubilee, 634 carats

Jonker, 726 carats

Imperial, 457 carats

all natural size

Some other diamonds famous enough to be given names came from the mines of India long before the African deposits were discovered. Most of these gems became the property of the rich and fabulous rajahs, the native rulers of India. Some are still in that country. The Koh-i-noor, most famous of the Indian stones, was known as early as 1300. In the century that followed, it passed back and forth from one conqueror to another—from the rajahs to the Mongols, from the Mongols to the Persians, and back to India again. Finally it passed to the British East India Company and was presented to Queen Victoria. It has been one of the crown jewels ever since.

India also produced the Blue Tavernier diamond, named after the great gem trader who found it. Somewhere in Iran today is the Darya-i-noor, another famous Indian stone, supposed to be the clearest and brightest diamond ever found. From India also came a 41-carat apple-green diamond, one of the rarest of its kind.

The earliest-known diamonds seem to have come from Central India near Golconda, a famous trading center. With the simple tools

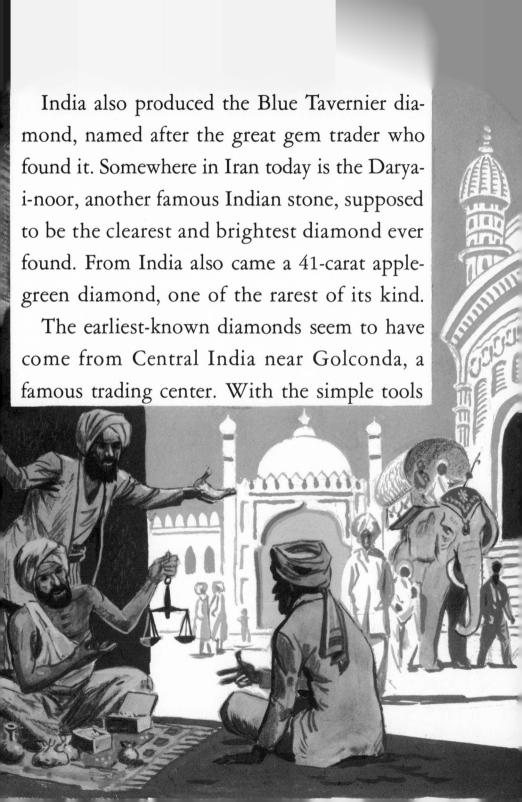

then available, these oriental stones were not cut well, and so they were not as striking or as brilliant as the diamonds you see today.

Diamonds gradually spread into Europe and by the 15th century both Antwerp and Amsterdam had become centers for the cutting of diamonds. The newer methods of cutting made diamonds more attractive, and the demand for them spread. Jean Baptiste Tavernier traveled through the Orient in 1665 and brought back records of the most famous oriental diamonds. Most of these had been found in the river gravels of India. These deposits were soon exhausted. By that time—1725—diamonds had been discovered in Brazil. For the next 150 years Brazil supplied many high-grade stones.

If you have ever picked up pebbles or pretty stones you will be happy to know that the great diamond mines in Africa were discovered in 1867 because a boy was doing exactly that. Erasmus Jacobs, a South African farmer's boy, brought home some glassy pebbles from along the Orange River, near Hopetown. A neighbor was attracted by one of the pebbles which the children were using in a game. He took it from one person to another till an expert pronounced

it a fine diamond. Two years later the same neighbor heard that a shepherd boy had another such pebble. He traded 500 sheep, 10 oxen, and a horse for it. This stone became the Star of South Africa, the first of the great African diamonds.

As the news spread, a diamond fever hit South Africa. Many mines were opened, and by the end of the century the region had yielded about 8 tons of rough stones. The first diamonds were found in river gravels; later they were traced to the Kimberley volcanic neck. This pipe, or neck, of volcanic rock, called peridotite, is the remains of an old volcano.

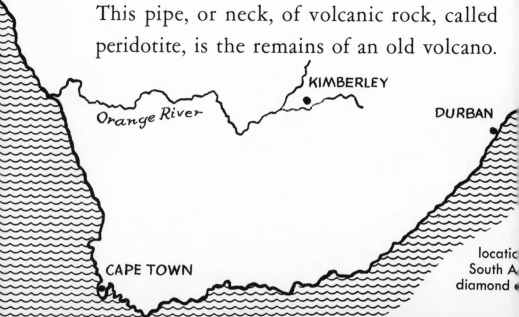

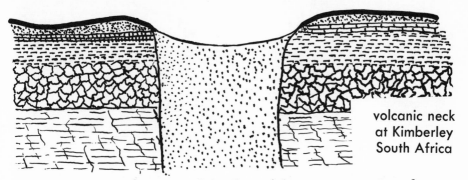

volcanic neck
at Kimberley
South Africa

Fragments of other kinds of lava are mixed with the diamond rock. The fresh, hard rock is bluish and so is called blue ground. Near the surface, where diamonds were first mined, the blue ground had been changed by the air and water into a soft yellowish rock, the yellow ground. At first, scores of small independent mines were dug, but as the mines grew deeper, cave-ins occurred. It was almost impossible to work safely or to get the ore out cheaply.

Kimberley mine
about 1875

modern shafts at
Kimberley mine

In 1889, Cecil Rhodes bought out the small
miners and, after a great financial battle, se-
cured control of the entire Kimberley deposit.
His company sunk shafts through the hard rock
near the pipe and then ran tunnels into the blue
ground, thus mining it cheaply and safely.

Blue ground was brought to the surface,
broken up, and spread on the ground. In six
months to a year, or perhaps two, the sunlight,
air, and rain caused a chemical breakdown. Finally the rock was soft enough for further
treatment. Nowadays blue ground is carefully
crushed, to avoid injuring the diamonds, and
is then hauled to the washing tables. Here it

flows over a series of boards covered with heavy grease. The rock particles and mud are carried off, but the diamonds stick to the grease and are collected.

In addition to the diamond fields at Kimberley and along the Vaal River, there are also diamond fields in other parts of South Africa, the Belgian Congo, Brazil, New South Wales, and Borneo. The old Indian deposits are no longer worked. Diamonds have also been found in Arkansas, and to some extent in British Guiana and Venezuela.

In North America there is only one spot like the blue-ground deposits of South Africa. This is at Murfreesboro, Pike County, Arkansas. Here peridotite rocks occur just as in Africa. The fresh rock is blue, but it turns yellow when weathered by the sun and rain.

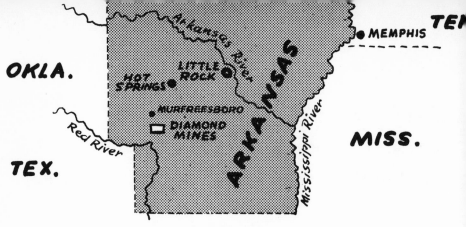

Diamonds were first found near Murfreesboro in 1906. During the next 10 or 15 years several mines were operated for short periods. All together, about 50,000 diamonds have been found, most of them small. They resemble Brazilian diamonds of good quality. The largest Arkansas stones have run from 14 to a big 40 carats. The faint-colored 40-carat diamond is the largest one ever found in America. The percentage of clear gem stones at Murfreesboro is high, but because most of the stones are small and not too plentiful, mining is costly. There is little chance that the Arkansas diamond deposit will ever become important.

Visitors to Murfreesboro pay a small fee and hunt for their own diamonds. It's fun, though the chances of finding a large gem are slim. Diamonds have also been found in dozens of other places in North America, but none of them have been found in their original rock. In no case have geologists been able to trace the diamonds to the place where they were formed.

Consider the large number of diamonds found all along the Great Lakes. Many have been found in Wisconsin, including the famous Eagle Diamond, weighing 16 carats. To the

Location of Great Lakes' diamond finds

south and east, diamonds have been found in Illinois, Indiana, and Ohio as far east as Cincinnati. About 50 or 60 diamonds have been found. Most of these were fairly large. Probably a great many smaller ones have escaped notice. All these stones were in debris pushed southward by a great glacier which covered the country 20,000 or more years ago. As the ice melted, sand, gravel, and mud mixed with it were dropped, and so were some diamonds.

Practically all the diamonds discovered have been found by accident. Most of the people who found them did not recognize them at once. They were attracted by the odd, greasy-looking pebbles and picked them up as something curious. Some diamonds remained around the house or in people's pockets for years before they were finally identified.

glacial scratches in polished rock

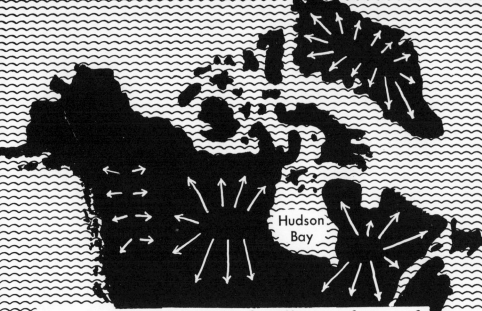

The glacier, which moved millions of tons of sand, gravel, and clay, left scratches and grooves in the bedrock as it passed. The direction of these shows which way the ice moved. Following the scratches northward, scientists have found that the ice formed at a number of centers. But all the diamonds have come from the ice which started west of Hudson Bay in Canada. This region has never been fully explored. Perhaps some day geologists will locate the diamond-bearing volcanic rock.

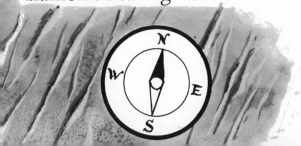

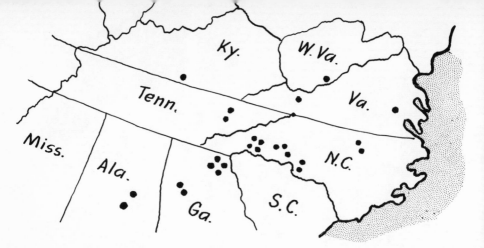

A similar mystery occurs in the Appalachian Mountains. Diamonds have been found in Georgia, North Carolina, Virginia, West Virginia, Kentucky, and Tennessee, but none in bedrock. The Appalachian Mountains are the oldest in North America; they have been worn down for many millions of years. Perhaps the original diamond rock no longer exists. But the diamonds scattered through these states prove that such a place did exist. Streams in the Appalachian Mountains could scarcely have carried the diamonds more than a hundred miles or so from where they were formed.

Among the Appalachian diamonds are some very interesting ones. The largest (32½ carats) was found by William Jones while he was pitching horseshoes in a vacant lot at Petersburg, West Virginia, in 1928. Not till 15 years later was the odd pebble identified as a diamond. Another Appalachian diamond weighed 24 carats, and several others weighing 2, 3, or 4 carats have been found.

A final source of diamonds is along our west coast. Diamonds were found in California during the Gold Rush. Several hundred have been dug up, mainly in the gold area. These were mostly quite small and not of very good color. Diamonds have also been found in the Rocky Mountains and in other scattered spots in the West. None of these finds were important, but the news of them kept people on edge during the 1870's, '80's, and '90's.

In 1872 two miners came into San Francisco with a bag of diamonds and other precious stones. Word of their find soon got around and

a number of leading bankers quickly investigated. Though the miners kept their claim a secret, they permitted it to be examined by an engineer hired by the bankers. He was led, blindfolded, from the railroad to the claim—a three-day trip. When the engineer returned, he told the bankers about the diamonds he personally had found. With great enthusiasm the bankers bought up the miners' claim and prepared to make a fortune.

But the head of the U. S. Geological Survey could not believe that his careful study of the western lands had failed to disclose diamond formations. He cross-examined the engineer and from details of his story figured out that the site of the deposit had to be in northern Colorado. Here the geologists went. They located an odd-shaped mountain the engineer had mentioned. Sure enough, they found a camp site, and soon began to find diamonds. However, it quickly became clear that the area had been salted: the diamonds were planted. They could never have been formed in the local rock. When this became known, the diamond bubble burst, but by that time, both "miners" had fled. Careful examination of the stones, which had fooled the engineer and the best jewelers in New York, showed that they were actually cheap, off-color diamonds from African mines—low-grade and of little value.

rough diamonds
5 times natural size

Nowadays such a fraud would not succeed. Experts know all about gem and industrial diamonds. Some can even tell, by its special characteristics, from what mine a particular diamond came. These characteristics, which fix the use and value of a diamond, include its variety, color, hardness, brilliance, and size.

Though all diamonds are chemically the same, there are several varieties that differ mainly in form and color. Besides gem stones there is the carbonado, a spongy black diamond from Brazil. The carbonado pebbles weigh up

carbonado

bort

to about two ounces. Some of them are harder than African bort. This is another kind of dark diamond of varying color and hardness. Bort usually occurs in the form of rough, round balls. Neither carbonado nor bort is a gem.

A gem diamond before it is cut is not an exciting stone. It may be dull, frosted, or waxy, tinged with yellow, brown, or blue. Sometimes it is a perfect eight-sided crystal. More often, it is imperfect and irregular.

diamond crystals

Diamonds have no color of their own. A pure diamond is as transparent as water. However, most stones do have color due to impurities. When the color is rich and bright, the diamonds are called fancy. Fancy diamonds may be blue, green, rich yellow or yellow-brown, pink, or even red. When the color is faint or of poor quality, the diamonds are called off-color diamonds. These may be a pale yellow, light brown, gray, or black, when unaltered carbon is present. Such diamonds are used in industry, because of their hardness. Gem diamonds are graded according to size, color, and clarity. Only the very best of them are cut, and polished, as gems.

sorting diamonds

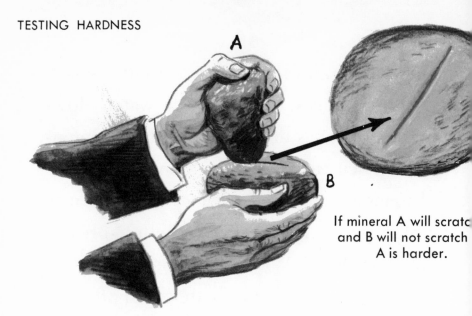

If mineral A will scratc
and B will not scratch
A is harder.

Hardness means resistance to scratching and indenting. Measuring hardness is a difficult matter. In 1822 Friedrich Mohs invented a scale to measure hardness. He used ten minerals, ranging from talc, the softest, to diamond, the hardest. But diamonds are so much harder than anything else that the upper end of the scale was incorrect. Later new steps were added to Mohs' scale, so that it now shows the hardness of diamonds more accurately.

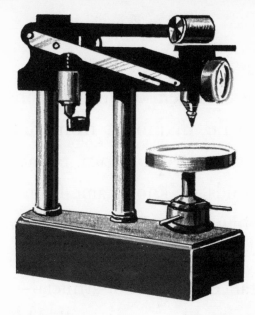

one type of machine
for measuring hardness
of metals

Old Mohs Scale	New Ridgway-Mohs Scale
1. talc	1. talc
2. gypsum	2. gypsum
3. calcite	3. calcite
4. fluorite	4. fluorite
5. apatite	5. apatite
6. orthoclase	6. orthoclase
	7. vitrious silica
7. quartz	8. quartz
8. topaz	9. topaz
	10. garnet
	11. fused zirconia or tantalum carbide
9. sapphire	12. fused alumina or tungsten carbide
	13. silicon carbide
	14. boron carbide
10. diamond	15. diamond

The hardness of gem-quality diamonds also varies. As a rule, diamonds from Brazil are harder than those from Africa. Some of the hardest diamonds we know came from a small deposit in New South Wales. All diamonds, however, are considerably harder than any other known substance—natural or artificial—except possibly a new synthetic stone called borozon. This seems to be as hard as a diamond.

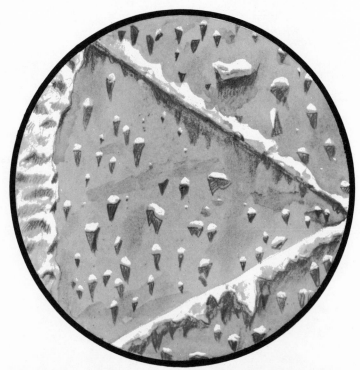

face of diamond crystal magnified 30,000 times

 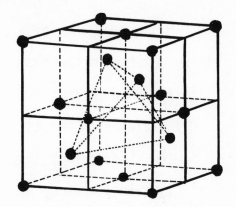

The reason why diamonds are so hard can be explained. Of all the atoms, carbon is the smallest. Each is connected to four other carbon atoms at a distance of 1.54 Angstrom Units, or six billionths of an inch. Each carbon atom has four chemical bonds, which link it to its neighbors in the strongest possible way. Finally, the diamond crystal, due to its cubic form, squeezes more chemical bonds into a given space than does any other substance. This gives diamonds their hardness and explains why nothing can be harder than a diamond.

Because of the arrangement of the bonds and the atoms in the crystals, diamonds are harder in one direction than another. Other minor differences between diamonds also make for slight differences in hardness.

The fact that a diamond is denser, or relatively heavier, than other forms of carbon shows that its atoms are packed more closely. If a piece of ordinary carbon weighs 1.5 ounces, a piece of graphite exactly the same size would weigh 2.5 ounces. A piece of bort would weigh about 3.4 ounces, and a gem-

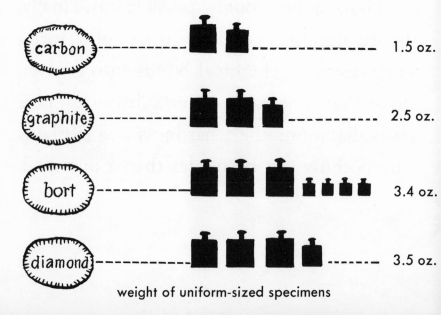

weight of uniform-sized specimens

quality diamond would weigh 3.5. This means that diamonds are over twice as heavy as ordinary carbon. There is only one possible explanation for this, since both are carbon. The diamond atoms are packed more tightly, with less space between them.

It's an old trick to put a penny in the bottom of a dish and make it pop into view. Get a friend to sight downward until the penny is hidden by the edge. Then all you need do is pour some water into the saucer, and your friend will see the penny reappear. The penny

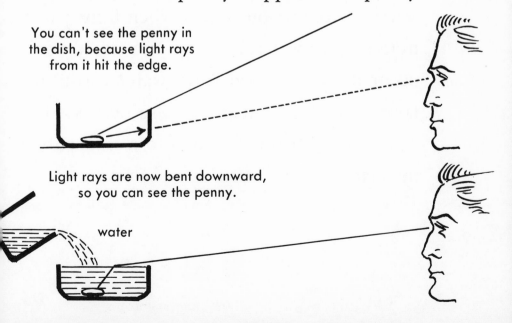

You can't see the penny in the dish, because light rays from it hit the edge.

Light rays are now bent downward, so you can see the penny.

water

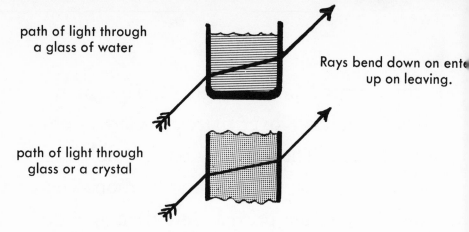

path of light through
a glass of water

Rays bend down on ent[e]
up on leaving.

path of light through
glass or a crystal

has not moved, but the layer of water has bent the rays of light coming from the penny to his eye. The light rays which formerly hit his forehead now hit his eye, and he can see the penny.

This bending of light as it passes from one transparent material into another is called refraction. Refraction occurs when light passes from air into water, or water into air. It would occur if light passed from water through a layer of transparent oil. It also occurs when light passes from the air into a transparent mineral or crystal, such as a diamond.

The measurement of refraction shows the amount of bending. This depends on the arrangement of atoms in the transparent substances, which slows down the speed of light. It is reported as a number called the index of refraction. The higher the index number, the more the light is refracted, or bent.

For most transparent minerals, the index of refraction is low. For water, it is 1.33; for glass, 1.5; for the emerald, 1.6. For the diamond, it is 2.5.

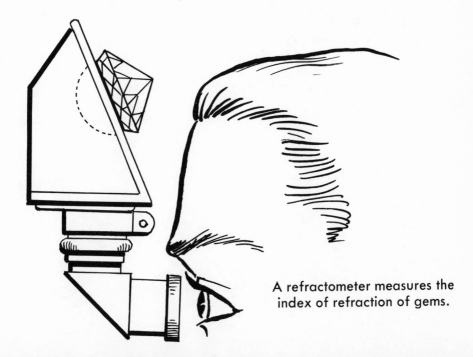

A refractometer measures the index of refraction of gems.

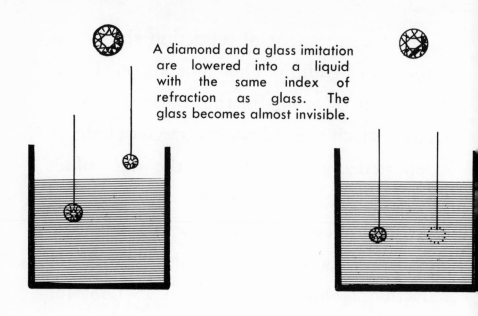

A diamond and a glass imitation are lowered into a liquid with the same index of refraction as glass. The glass becomes almost invisible.

Sometimes a gem is made of a thin layer of diamond cemented to glass.

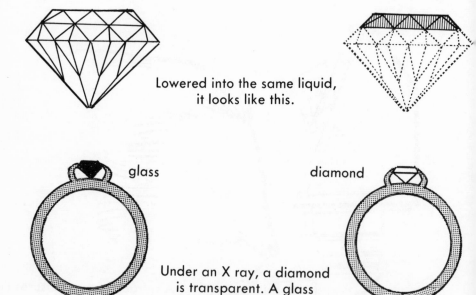

Lowered into the same liquid, it looks like this.

glass   diamond

Under an X ray, a diamond is transparent. A glass imitation is not.

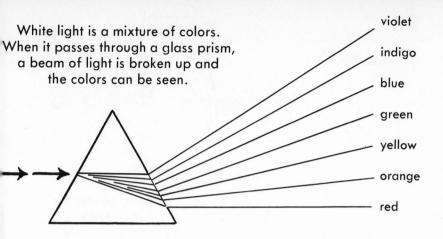

White light is a mixture of colors. When it passes through a glass prism, a beam of light is broken up and the colors can be seen.

violet
indigo
blue
green
yellow
orange
red

The index of refraction varies slightly with the color of the light or, more accurately, with its wave length. Some minerals will spread, or disperse, more light than others. The diamond is such a mineral, and hence the light coming from a diamond because of refraction exhibits all the colors of the rainbow, because of dispersal.

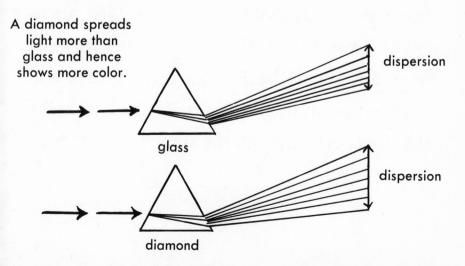

A diamond spreads light more than glass and hence shows more color.

dispersion

glass

dispersion

diamond

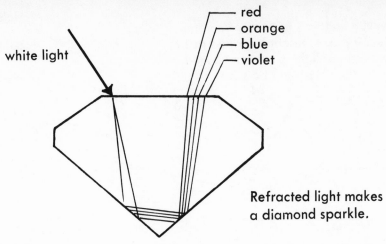

white light

red
orange
blue
violet

Refracted light makes
a diamond sparkle.

A diamond is brilliant, after it is cut. It sparkles and glitters because of refraction and dispersal of light. A few other minerals, such as titania and the zircon, have an even higher index of refraction than the diamond. They are also used as gems, though they are not as valuable as diamonds.

To take advantage of the high index of refraction of diamonds, many gems are cut in such a way that light passing into them is bent completely back toward the source and does not go through the side or the bottom of the stone, even though the stone is transparent.

To make this happen, the facets or faces of the diamond are cut at an angle of about 24 degrees. The most common cut for diamonds is called the brilliant. This style of cutting results in 58 facets. There are several kinds of brilliant cuts—some simple, some more complex. But the best-known cut produces a stone that is flat on the top, widens, and then comes to a point at the back.

CUTS OF DIAMOND

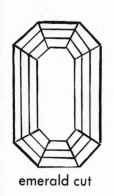

emerald cut

marquise cut

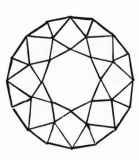

brilliant cut

pendeloque or
pear-shaped

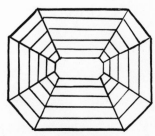

step cut

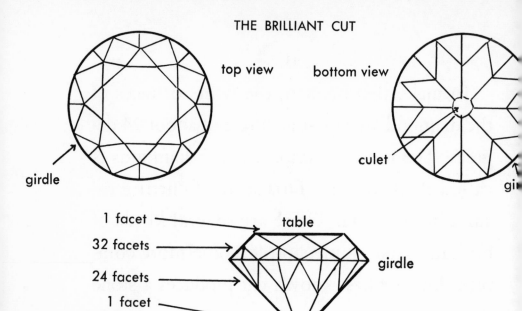

top view   bottom view

girdle

culet

gi

1 facet — table
32 facets —
24 facets —
1 facet —
total, 58 facets

girdle

culet

side view

The flat top of a brilliant is called a table. It has 8 sides. Sloping from each side are 8 triangular facets. Against these, 4 main facets and 4 corner facets are cut, and then 16 small facets. Now the stone is at its widest point, which is called the girdle. As it starts to slant sharply back, more facets are cut along the slope.

Diamond cutting demands great skill and patience. Diamonds often show signs of internal strain. This strain may appear in the form of flaws, or spots, where the diamonds do not have a good grain and therefore break unevenly. Diamonds may also contain tiny gas bubbles. For these and other reasons diamonds sometimes actually explode when cut. One 12-carat diamond was completely ruined this way.

stages in cutting a brilliant

crystal　　　　1　　　　2

3　　　　4　　　　5

6　　　　7　　　　8

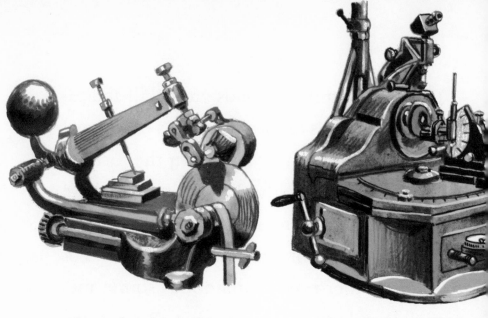

diamond-sawing machine   automatic diamond polisher

Diamonds can be "bruted" (rubbed), or split. They can be sawed with a thin disc carrying diamond dust. Once this was done by hand and with simple equipment. Now machine power and ingenious inventions take care of the routine work of cutting and polishing diamonds. Yet only the expert's skill and judgment can get the best gem from a rough stone, and get rid of flaws with the smallest loss.

The value of diamonds also depends on their size. Less than one fifth of the diamonds found are of gem quality, and the number of top-quality gems is much less. Besides, in cutting a diamond at least half of the stone is lost. Depending on its shape and form, it takes a rough gem stone of 1 to 1.5 carats to yield a half-carat brilliant.

steps in cutting Uncle Sam,
the largest diamond found in the U.S.

as found
40.2 car.

30 car.

22.8 car.

14.3 car.

final cut stone,
12.4 car.

THE VALUE OF DIAMONDS INCREASES GREATLY WITH SIZE.

(average value of first-quality gems)

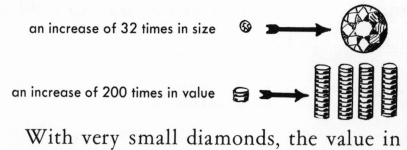

¼ carat	½ carat	1 carat	2 carats	4 carats	8 carats
$200	$400	$1300	$4000	$12,000	$40,000

an increase of 32 times in size

an increase of 200 times in value

With very small diamonds, the value increases directly with the weight, but with gems of a carat or more, doubling the weight will increase the value at least three or four times. Large perfect stones are so rare that they are worth a fortune. But neither the beauty of diamonds nor their rarity can completely account for the value of these gems.

Soon after diamond mining moved into the control of large companies, these firms joined together to form an organization, or syndicate, to sell their stones. For over 70 years nearly all the diamonds mined were sold by this group. The diamond syndicate grew and took in new producers as soon as their mines became important. Today this group sells about 97 per cent of the world's diamonds. The supply and the prices are controlled, keeping the diamond market steady and the price up. This kind of control, known as monopoly, affects both gems and industrial diamonds.

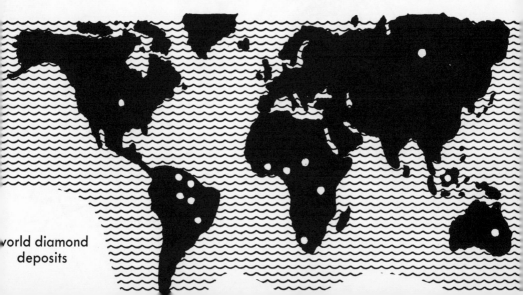

world diamond
deposits

The most important diamonds, however, are those you never see. They are not in rings or necklaces, but in factories. Even here they are not easily found, because diamonds are used only in the best cutting tools.

Industrial diamonds have thousands of uses. In homes they make the needles of hi-fi phonograph pickups. In the oil fields they crown the great rotary bits which cut down through solid rock a mile or more in search of oil.

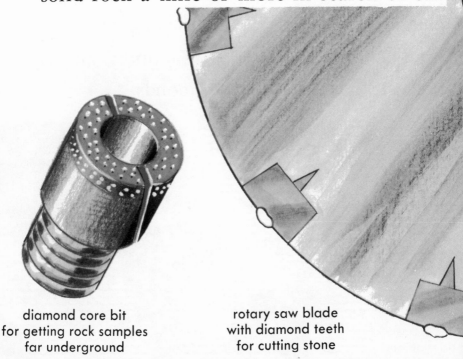

diamond core bit
for getting rock samples
far underground

rotary saw blade
with diamond teeth
for cutting stone

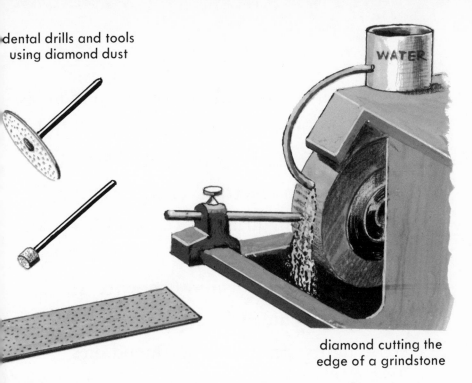

dental drills and tools using diamond dust

diamond cutting the edge of a grindstone

Your dentist uses diamonds too—often as a powder cemented to paper or a wheel. Diamond wheels cut and polish other stones and many metals. They cut metal parts smoothly and accurately for all engines from automobiles' to rockets'. And when diamonds are not used directly for cutting, they are used to make the carbide grinding and polishing wheels which are more commonly used.

Most marvelous of all are the diamond dies
—flat diamonds through which small holes
have been accurately drilled with another diamond or by an electrical charge. These diamonds are of gem quality, except for their color.
Metal pulled through the holes in the hard
diamond is drawn out into fine wire. All electrical equipment, including the filaments of
electric lights, depends on diamond dies.

two types of diamond dies   diamond die mounted in bra

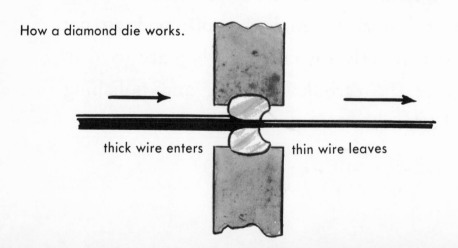

How a diamond die works.

thick wire enters   thin wire leaves

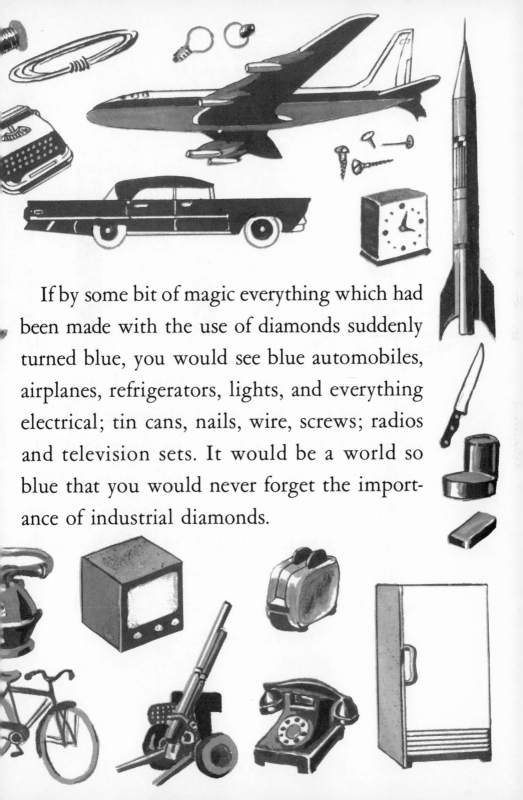

If by some bit of magic everything which had been made with the use of diamonds suddenly turned blue, you would see blue automobiles, airplanes, refrigerators, lights, and everything electrical; tin cans, nails, wire, screws; radios and television sets. It would be a world so blue that you would never forget the importance of industrial diamonds.

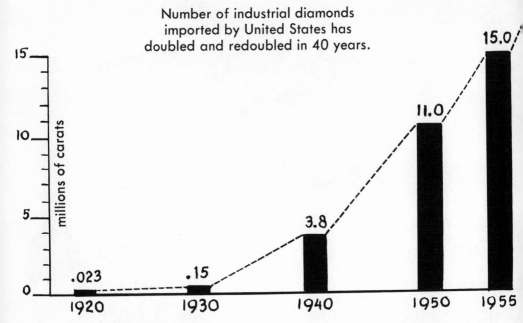

Number of industrial diamonds imported by United States has doubled and redoubled in 40 years.

millions of carats

15

10

5

0

.023   .15   3.8   11.0   15.0

1920   1930   1940   1950   1955

The need for diamonds in industry is so great that there has never been enough of them to meet the demand. The production of diamonds has gone up and up till it is now about 25 million carats a year—and over 80 per cent of these are industrial diamonds. Each year the United States uses more and more diamonds— now about 16 million carats a year. Till recently, all were imported.

Because of the great value of diamonds, the idea of making them artificially first occurred long ago, even before people knew what diamonds really were, or what forces were necessary to produce them. The first attempt to make diamonds was in the Middle Ages, when

alchemist in his laboratory

alchemists were also trying to make gold from lead. Many alchemists were frauds, but others sincerely tried, with no success, to produce gold or diamonds. A few did make important scientific discoveries along the way.

A little over 100 years ago, more serious attempts were made. There were many failures, but the great French chemist Moissan dissolved carbon in molten iron. Then, by sudden cooling, he produced tremendous pressure. Testing the iron convinced Moissan that he had made

Moissan tried to make artificial diamonds.

microscopic diamonds. But new calculations of the heat and pressure reached make it seem that Moissan did not get diamonds at all, but merely some white, transparent impurity.

After all the trials and failures, artificial diamonds were finally made, but not until 1954. Then, at the General Electric Research laboratories, Dr. Herbert M. Strong put carbon in a new thousand-ton press and kept it under a pressure of some 800,000 pounds per square inch.

conference on superpressure in General Electric
laboratory

diamond phonograph needle

head of a pin
same magnification

largest of the first
synthetic diamonds

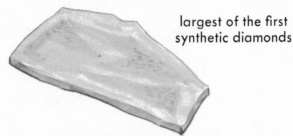

actual
length
of this diamond

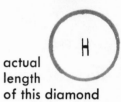

When the press was opened, the material was cut away with grindstones, but the center part was too hard to cut. When this was tested, it proved capable of scratching sapphires. Soon it was clear that at last a diamond had been made artificially. These experiments have been repeated hundreds of times. The crystals that form have been checked with X rays, by the degree of their hardness, and in all other known ways. It is now certain, beyond any doubt, that they are diamonds.

The synthetic diamonds made so far are not of gem quality. They are grayish black in color, and the larger stones are only about the size of a grain of salt. A heap of synthetic diamonds looks like a pile of coarse coal dust, but each grain can be put to industrial use.

typical man-made diamonds
magnified 40 times

the first batch of
synthetic diamonds,
worth about $30,000

In the two years after the first synthetic diamonds were made, over 100,000 carats of industrial diamonds were produced. General Electric believes it can manufacture three and a half million carats of diamonds every year. However, this will be less than half of the needed supply of industrial stones.

To make artificial diamonds, a combination of very high pressure and very high temperature is needed. Scientists had created pressures of well over a million pounds per square inch. They had obtained temperatures of about ten thousand degrees Fahrenheit—the temperature at the surface of the sun. But never had the high temperatures and high pressures been produced together, except for a very short period of time, as in an explosion.

Recently a new kind of hydraulic press was developed. It can operate on pressures of over a million and a half pounds per square inch. In it, temperatures up to about 5000 degrees Fahrenheit can be held for a long time. This combination made the manufacture of artificial diamonds possible.

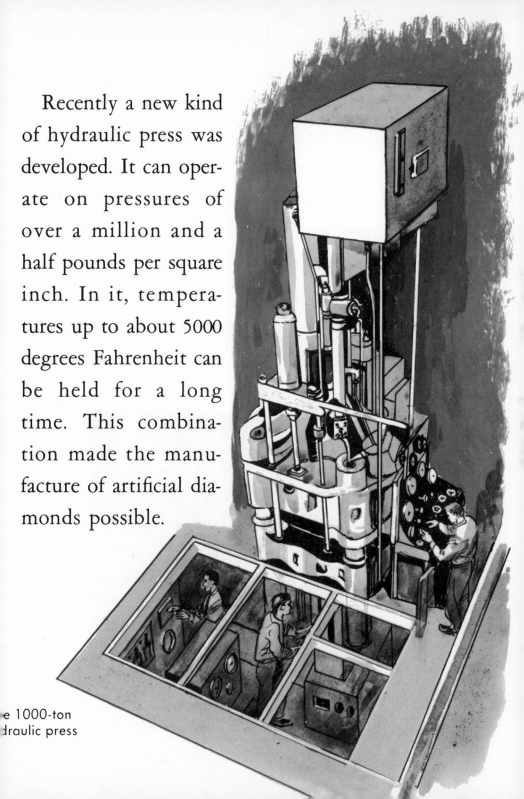

e 1000-ton
draulic press

From the careful study of graphite, diamonds, and other forms of carbon, scientists worked out a diagram which indicated roughly the conditions that would be needed to produce each type. Studies showed that the molecules forming in the graphite pattern are the most stable. Because of this, a great deal of energy is needed to make them rearrange themselves in the diamond pattern. On the other hand, be-

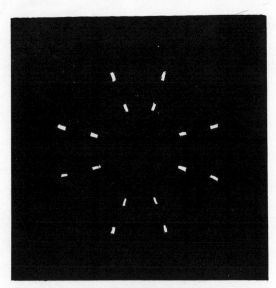

X-ray photograph of
diamond showing
simple crystal pattern

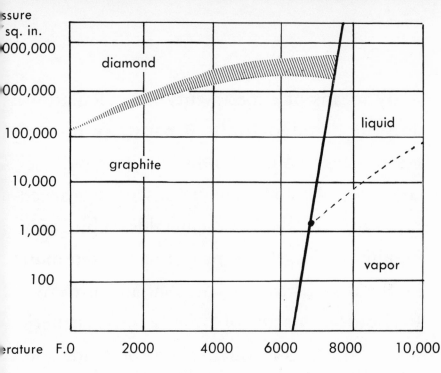

cause graphite is the more stable of the two, it is fairly easy to change diamonds back into graphite. When a diamond is heated to higher than 900 degrees centigrade, the change takes place. At higher temperatures, diamonds will change to graphite more rapidly. Diamonds will also burn when hot enough. In burning, they produce carbon-dioxide gas, exactly as if charcoal or some other form of carbon was being burned.

By means of experiments and calculations and the detailed study of naturally formed gems, scientists now know the diamond's secrets. Not too long ago chemists first learned how to make synthetic emeralds, rubies, and sapphires. They have made a half-dozen more synthetic gems that are brilliant and attractive. It is only a matter of time before synthetic diamonds of gem quality will be made too. But even when that day comes, natural diamonds will still be the best liked and most treasured of all the gems.

synthetic emerald
sapphires, rubie

1902

synthetic
gem diamonds

196?